LILLENAS DRAMA

Sketches for the
Christian Walk

Body,

D1611507

Mind,

and

Spirit

by Jeff Smith

Lillenas PUBLISHING COMPANY

KANSAS CITY, MO 64141

Questions? Please write or call:
Lillenas Publishing Company
Drama Resources
P.O. Box 419527
Kansas City, MO 64141
Phone: 816-931-1900 ● Fax: 816-753-4071
E-mail: drama@lillenas.com
Web: www.lillenas.com/drama

Cover art by Kevin Williamson

Dedication

This collection of sketches is lovingly dedicated to
my friends, **Fred** and **Mary Pfister** whose *words* have been
an inspiration, whose *ways* have been a godly example,
and whose *wit* and *wisdom* have made for
a great story and many fond memories.
Thank you for sharing your lives with us.

Contents

Preface

I've always been a runner—high school track, 10K races, marathons, miles and miles of jogging trails. I race my boys out the door to the car; I bound up steps; I catch myself walking ahead of my wife. I'm always on the go, and there's only one speed . . . fast. So, the idea of the Christian "walk" is as foreign a metaphor to me as "whiter than snow" might be to a native of the Bahamas. Even though Paul uses the word "walk" many times in describing the Christian experience, I prefer his admonition in 1 Corinthians 9:24b, "Run [the race] in such a way as to get the prize." Maybe it's that archaic, cave-dwelling "man thing," but the concept of a race works better for three reasons:

- The *pace of the race* keeps my **BODY** strong
- The *purpose of the race* keeps my **MIND** focused
- The *passion of the race* keeps my **SPIRIT** fired up

Body, Mind, and Spirit—this collection is a reflection of people, places, and stories that have helped shape my Christian "walk" on the "run."

Body, Mind, and Spirit

Theme: Being led by the Spirit of God

Scripture: "For the sinful nature desires what is contrary to the Spirit, and the Spirit what is contrary to the sinful nature. They are in conflict with each other, so that you do not do what you want" (Galatians 5:17).

Cast:
> BODY: *M/F; lazy, impatient, irritable*
> MIND: *M/F; pompous, analytical, meticulous*
> SPIRIT: *M/F; energized, uplifted, bright, bubbly*

Setting: Everyman's house in the morning.

Running Time: 5 minutes

Production Note: All movements, although not specifically directed, should be synchronized unless otherwise indicated, reflecting the movements of one person. We break out of this mode later in the script as the struggle for control becomes more intense. All props are pantomimed.

(BODY, MIND, *and* SPIRIT *lay side-to-side with their feet toward the audience. A bedside alarm goes off. All reach for the alarm clock, sit up, rub eyes, yawn, and stretch.)*

SPIRIT: Bless the Lord, oh, my soul. Let all that is within me praise His name.

MIND: I've got to get up and get started here. Such a busy day with so much to do. Now where did I put that list . . .

BODY: But it would be nice to catch a few more winks before work. I have 15 minutes before I have to be up.

(All lay back down. Beat. SPIRIT *sits up.)*

SPIRIT: A little sleep, a little slumber, a little folding of the hands to rest, and poverty will come in on you like a bandit. This is the day that the Lord has made, let us rejoice and be glad in it.

MIND *(sitting up):* There is so much to do. I need those extra 15 minutes to get on top of things this morning. I don't want to miss breakfast.

BODY *(sitting up):* Breakfast? I'll get up for breakfast. I can have leftover pizza from the party last night, and I could probably dig up another Pepsi somewhere.

SPIRIT *(to* BODY): Man does not live by bread . . . or pizza . . . alone. But instead, by every word that comes from the mouth of God.

(All pick up a nearby Bible and open it.)

SPIRIT *(continues):* Consider the lilies of the field. They do not labor or spin. Yet, I tell you, not even Solomon in all his splendor was dressed like one of these . . .

*(*MIND *looks away from Bible.)*

MIND: I have that business meeting with old Farnsworth today. He's such a miser. I better dress conservatively if I want to get that sale. Perhaps the pinstripe gray with the white shirt! *(Remembering)* Oh, that shirt has a hole in it.

BODY: If it's holy, let Spirit wear it.

*(*BODY *laughs as* SPIRIT *gives both a cool glance.)*

SPIRIT *(clears throat; others get Bible back into position):* Rather, clothe yourself with the Lord Jesus Christ and do not think how to gratify the desires of the flesh . . .

BODY *(looking away from Bible):* There was a brownie down there. I know I saw a brownie. I could have pizza, pop, and a brownie.

SPIRIT: Don't you know that you are the temple of the Most High? You are not your own. You were bought and paid for with a price.

BODY: OK. OK. So we'll have an apple and some grapes. You're into fruit, right, Spirit? *(Laughs at joke as* SPIRIT *rolls his [her] eyes and shakes head.)*

MIND *(looks at watch):* Look at the time. I must get going here.

*(*BODY *and* MIND *put Bible down and try to walk away, but* SPIRIT *doesn't move, making it appear that* BODY *and* MIND *are stuck in their places.)*

BODY: We have to get a shower. We don't want an unclean Spirit now, do we? An unclean Spirit has no inheritance in the kingdom of God.

SPIRIT: But we forgot to . . .

MIND: Put out the garbage last night. I can't believe I forgot that. Come on, let's go.

*(*SPIRIT *reluctantly closes Bible, puts it down, and moves off with* BODY *and* MIND. *They move in a circle around the playing space as they talk.)*

SPIRIT: Well, let's sing to the Lord this morning. It is good to praise the Lord and make music to Him.

*(*SPIRIT *starts to sing "Jesus Loves Me."* BODY, *who has been dragging around the circle, moves out of the group.)*

BODY: I'm sick of that mellow gospel garbage. I want to rock and roll.

*(*BODY *lets out a scream and starts belting out "I Feel Good" with a James Brown impersonation on air guitar.* MIND, *letting down his [her] guard, starts dancing.* SPIRIT *stands between them, aghast. As* SPIRIT *tries to get control over the next*

section, Body *sings louder,* Mind *continues dancing.* Spirit *speaks over the din—the movements and music become constrained until they are both still and quiet.)*

Spirit: Finally, brethren, whatever is true, whatever is noble, whatever is right, whatever is pure, lovely or admirable, think about these things.

(If necessary, Spirit *can repeat this verse until* Mind *and* Body *are under control.* Mind *and* Body *look at* Spirit.*)*

Body/Mind *(singsongy):* Every party has a pooper—that's why we invited *you.* Party pooper. Super dooper.

(All stare forward as if looking in a bathroom mirror. Synchronized movements can be added here.)

Body: A zit! A zit on my nose.

Mind: Too much Pepsi, you imbecile.

Body: Aren't you the one who is supposed to say when we've had enough? And I'm supposed to go out with Wanda tonight; the most fabulous babe in all the world. And now I've got a zit on my nose.

Mind: What about Farnsworth? How am I going to make a sale to Farnsworth with a zit on my nose? He won't listen to me. He'll be looking at my nose. He won't hear a word I am saying.

Spirit: What is man that you are mindful of him? The son of man that you care for him?

Mind/Body: Shut up!

Mind: We're talking big bucks here.

Body: We're talking fabulous babes here.

Mind *(to* Body): You shut up too. It's all your fault. How could you be so stupid?

Spirit: The sinful mind is hostile toward God. It does not submit to God's law, nor can it do so.

Mind *(to* Body): All this commotion has put us way behind schedule. There is still so much to do. We'll barely have time for breakfast. Come on, let's go.

*(*Spirit *and* Body *fall in behind* Mind *and walk in a circle.)*

Body *(in cadence with steps):* I want pizza! I want pizza.

(Repeated, getting louder, until they reach "kitchen." Stop and turn front.)

Mind: All right, but only because it's quick and easy.

Body: . . . and Pepsi!

Mind: No! You've had your way, and now look at us. Come on, let's eat.

*(*Body *and* Mind *reach for food in front of them.* Spirit *resists.)*

Spirit *(clears throat):* Aren't you forgetting something?

Body: Uggghh. Don't you ever take a break? *(Bow heads to pray)* Over the lips and through the gums, look out tummy 'cause here it comes!

(All are caught up by Body, *who starts inhaling food.)*

MIND: Hey, slow down! It's not going to run away. We shouldn't eat so fast . . .

BODY: Pepsi, Pepsi, Pepsi . . .

MIND: You are *not* having Pepsi.

BODY: I want Pepsi. I want Pepsi . . .

(Ad-libbing continues between BODY *and* MIND, *escalating into a shouting match for control.* SPIRIT *is caught in the middle and bows his [her] head to pray. Finally,* SPIRIT *whistles, blows a whistle, or yells to get control.* SPIRIT *takes a more militant approach toward others, lining them up and addressing them as a drill sergeant would address recruits.)*

SPIRIT: Attention! (BODY *and* MIND *jump to military position of attention.)* I'm going to be in charge of this person today, and I say live by the Spirit so that you don't gratify the desires *(to* BODY's *face)* of the body. For the body desires what is contrary to the Spirit. Now, let's knock out a prayer.

BODY *(underneath breath):* Oh man, I hate to pray.

SPIRIT: At ease, Body, or I'll send you on a three-day fast. Now we *pray.* (SPIRIT *leads in a moment of silent prayer.)* Amen. Now we're ready to face the day. Fall in . . . (BODY *jumps in front of* SPIRIT.) *Behind me!*

*(*BODY *whimpers and moves behind* SPIRIT. MIND *is already there and motions* BODY *to move to the end of the line.* MIND *snickers. As* SPIRIT *leads them away, they sing "Onward, Christian Soldiers."* BODY *and* MIND *continue to quarrel and pick at each other as they exit.)*

The Lost and Found Shop

Theme: Evangelism. We are commanded to share the gospel message with a lost and dying world. Why do we "hold on" to truth that has been revealed to us, by grace, as if it were ours to keep?

Scripture: Luke 15; Matthew 5:13-16; 28:19-21

Cast:

NARRATOR: *male or female*

SHOP OWNER [SO]: *middle-aged male [female]. Tends the shop as work that has to be done as opposed to something he [she] enjoys doing. Actions/reactions are always very "put upon." Antagonistic toward the Narrator.*

SHEPHERD: *male, untidy, dirty; biblical dress*

WOMAN: *40-50ish; biblical dress*

FATHER: *40-50ish; biblical dress; sad and slow*

Setting: A shack (SR) that resembles a child's lemonade stand. Think in terms of Lucy's psychiatrist's stand in "Peanuts." There is a sign atop the stand that says Lost and Found.

Running Time: 6 minutes

(NARRATOR *stands SL. As he [she] begins to read,* SHOP OWNER [SO] *enters vendor's shack and prepares for the day's "business." SO puts on a clerk's apron and straightens a few pamphlets, books, etc., strewn across the stand. SO may take a rag and wipe off some of the products. The last thing done before sitting down and opening pages of a tabloid [The Star] is to hang a sign that states Open for Ministry with the word "Ministry" crossed out and "Business" written below or beside it.)*

NARRATOR: Now the tax collectors and the sinners were all gathered around to hear Jesus speak. But the Pharisees and the teachers of the Law muttered, "This man welcomes sinners and eats with them." Then Jesus told them a parable. Suppose one of you has a hundred sheep and loses one of them . . .

(SHEPHERD *enters and moves toward the Lost and Found stand. He is dirty and disheveled. He also appears a bit distressed. SO tries to ignore him by pulling the tabloid up over his [her] face.* SHEPHERD *clears his throat. SO finally acknowledges him, with a sigh.)*

13

SO: Yeah?

SHEPHERD: I'm looking for a sheep.

SO: And . . .

SHEPHERD: He's, uh . . . white. (SO *rolls eyes.*) And fluffy . . .

SO: Does your sheep have a name?

SHEPHERD: Harry.

SO: Harry?

SHEPHERD: We named him after an uncle.

SO: Harry.

SHEPHERD *(nods):* Yeah.

(SO *sighs, shakes head, and exits.*)

SHEPHERD *(to* NARRATOR*):* My Uncle Harry had a little nose that always seemed to be running because of allergies. (NARRATOR *nods.*) He's really a very good animal. Um, Harry . . . my sheep, I mean. *(Looks away sadly)* I'm not sure what happened.

NARRATOR: Sheep can do stupid things.

SHEPHERD: I've got to find him.

NARRATOR: I'm sure the Shop Owner will help you.

SO *(enters, moves behind counter):* No sheep answering to the name "Harry."

SHEPHERD: Oh, he only answers to my voice. Perhaps I could go and . . .

SO *(abruptly):* No Harry Sheep. *(Picks up tabloid and begins reading)*

SHEPHERD: Oh. All right . . . um . . . *(Begins to exits, then returns)* I'm not sure where to look from here. Any suggestions?

SO *(speaks from behind tabloid):* Try calling 1-800-CRY-WOLF, or you might try shepherdlink.com. They may be able to help.

(SHEPHERD *shakes head and exits.*)

NARRATOR: Why didn't you let him look?

SO: Did you see the way he was dressed?

NARRATOR: He's a shepherd.

SO: That's not an excuse for being a slob.

NARRATOR: You're judging him by what he was wearing?

SO: He smelled bad too.

NARRATOR: That's no reason to turn him away without help.

SO: I prefer to think of it as business savvy . . . years of experience. I didn't get this far by doling out lost items to every Bildad, Eliphaz, and Zophar who show up looking for a free handout.

NARRATOR: But . . .

SO *(sharply):* Don't you have something to be reading?

NARRATOR *(shakes head, reads):* Ah, suppose a woman has 10 silver coins and loses 1.

(WOMAN *enters, distressed and a bit disheveled. She is a little more demonstrative.)*

WOMAN: Please, please can you help me?

SO *(putting down paper):* I can try.

WOMAN: I've lost a very precious silver coin. I have looked everywhere.

SO: What kind of coin did you say it was?

WOMAN: Uh, silver . . . coin.

SO: Where do you think you lost this "precious" memento?

WOMAN: Somewhere near my home in the city.

SO: Well, the "city" is a very big place. But we did have a silver coin returned.

WOMAN *(relieved):* Oh, thank heavens! It was part of a wedding present from my father. So, it has sentimental value too. Please give it to me.

SO *(tallying a bill on a pad):* Let's see . . . that will be one silver coin.

WOMAN: For what?

SO: Finder's fee.

NARRATOR: You didn't find it!

SO: Commission.

NARRATOR: Commission? It is the value of the coin.

WOMAN: This is outrageous.

SO: Perhaps you might want to take your grievance to the Better Business Bureau. We also have a complaint box. You could fill out a card and . . .

WOMAN *(running off stage):* Oh, my coin; my precious silver coin. What will I do . . . ?

NARRATOR *(incredulous):* You were rude to that woman.

SO: I was professional. We're a lost and found, not a daycare for people who can't watch after themselves.

NARRATOR: You stole that woman's coin.

SO: I happen to know that woman has not paid a cent of tax on that money.

NARRATOR: It was a gift.

SO: Listen! You're the Narrator. You don't dictate policy. Just do your job and I'll do mine, OK?

NARRATOR *(shaking head, returns to position):* Once there was a farmer who had two sons. The younger one said to his father, "Father, give me my share of the estate." So, he divided his property between them. Not long after that, the younger son got together all he had and set off for a distant country. There he squandered his inheritance.

(An older man enters. He is not as "alarmed" as the first two. Still, he is worn and worried.)

FATHER: My son is missing.

SO: Sir, we're not the police department. We're the lost and found.

FATHER: Oh. OK, then he's lost.

SO: Can you identify him?

FATHER: It's been over a year since he left, but I'm sure I'll recognize him.

SO: Over a year?

(FATHER *sadly nods head.*)

SO *(pulling out a document on a clipboard):* Well, I'm sorry sir, but our policy explicitly states that any property not recovered within a year becomes the property of the Lost and Found.

FATHER: But he's my son.

SO *(pushing clipboard toward him across counter):* You need to read the fine print, sir.

(NARRATOR *is furious and moves to Lost and Found to intervene on the man's behalf.*)

NARRATOR: You *don't* understand.

SO *(confrontational):* You'd be surprised.

NARRATOR: This man is the boy's father.

SO: I know the story as well as you do.

NARRATOR: You have an obligation.

SO: I work within the rules.

NARRATOR: You call and get that boy here! NOW!

SO: You're not my boss.

NARRATOR: But I know your boss . . . very well. I have stood here and watched you deny these people what belongs to them because of your bias, greed, laziness, and bogus rules. Now, you call . . . or I will.

(Beat)

SO *(picking up phone, dials):* Hello? Social Services? Yes, I'd like to report a negligent and abusive father . . .

NARRATOR: No!

FATHER: I don't understand this. I just don't understand . . . *(Exits, head in hands, walking aimlessly off stage.* NARRATOR *grabs phone from* SO *and slams receiver down.)*

NARRATOR: Give me that! I can't believe this.

SO *(looks at watch):* Oh my. Look at the time. *(Reaches to turn over sign Open for Business. It says OUT TO LUNCH. Exits as* NARRATOR *tries to stop him [her].)*

NARRATOR: Wait. You can't just leave like that! Get back here. *(Watches him [her] depart in disbelief. Turns back toward stand and notices the sign. Holds it up to make a point.)* Hmmph. "Out to Lunch." Ain't that the truth. *(Shakes head. Exits.)*

The God Pound

Theme: Witnessing

Scripture: "In the same way, let your light shine before men, that they may see your good deeds and praise your Father in heaven" (Matthew 5:16).

Cast:

> JANELLE: *20+ female, sweet and sensitive. "God-owner" who is bringing her "God" to the God Pound.*
>
> TORRY: *50+ female, crusty and insensitive. She has worked in the Pound for many years, taking care of the "Gods" and has been "hardened" by the way seemingly loving "God-owners" treat their Gods.*

Setting: A counter with a sign on a nearby wall that says God Pound. On the counter are administrative items like papers, clipboard, file folders, etc. There is also a counter bell for service.

Running Time: 5 minutes

(JANELLE *enters the scene "walking" a "dog" on a "leash." These actions/items are mimed. She talks to the "dog" as she enters the scene.*)

JANELLE: Good God. That's a nice boy. What a good God you are. *(Walks to the counter)* Sit, God. Good boy. *("Pats" the "dog" and looks around for assistance.)* Hello? *(Pause)* Hello? *(Rings bell)*

TORRY *(offstage):* I'm comin' already. *(Enters scene carrying a bucket in one hand and a mop in the other. She puts the bucket down and sets the mop in the bucket. Speaks without looking up.)* Whatcha got?

JANELLE: I wanted to see about gettin' my God . . .

TORRY *(moving to counter and "sizing up" the situation):* New God owner?

JANELLE: About a month and a half . . .

TORRY: Just a pup. Hmmph. *(Shakes her head)*

JANELLE: He's a handful. *(To "dog")* Come back here. Sit. Behave, God!

TORRY: Let me guess . . . You got him at a retreat, and now he's getting to be a little more than you bargained for, huh?

JANELLE: Well, not exactly. *(Yanks on rope again)* Stay, God. Good God.

TORRY: I know the story. They're cute when they're pups. Everyone else is gettin' them and cryin' over their little Gods. So you think you just got to have one too. All that huggin' and cryin' just makes you lose yer senses, I s'pose. Next thing you know they're breakin' things and leaving messes everywhere.

JANELLE: No. He really has been no bother.

TORRY *(taking out a pad and pencil)*: How long you leavin' him?

JANELLE: Just the weekend.

TORRY *(writing)*: Hmmph. Weekend, huh?

JANELLE: Well, yes, I . . .

TORRY: Where are ya goin'?

JANELLE: I . . .

TORRY: Let me guess. *(Leans over counter and takes hold of* JANELLE's *hand, inspecting it)* You're not married?

JANELLE *(taken aback)*: No, no . . .

TORRY *(releasing* JANELLE's *hand)*: Boyfriend comin' in for the weekend and he doesn't like Gods?

JANELLE *(to "dog")*: God, be quiet. Sit. *(To* TORRY*)* How did you know?

TORRY: Typical.

JANELLE: Listen, I just want to . . .

TORRY: None of my business. Just seems a little crazy to get a God at all if you're going to keep him cooped up in here all the time.

JANELLE: Oh no, no. It's just a couple of days and . . .

TORRY: The first time.

JANELLE: What?

TORRY: The second and third time it'll be another day. Then after that, you'll start to leave him here a little longer . . . until finally you're just visitin', if at all.

JANELLE: Oh no, it's just a couple of days, really. I just need to sort things out with this guy, and I don't want any . . . distractions.

TORRY: You seem nice enough. But I'm tellin' ya that this pound is filled up with Gods just like yours. I know how it goes.

JANELLE *(looking at "dog")*: What happens to them?

TORRY: Hmmph. They just sit and wait for someone to come and visit.

JANELLE: God-owners?

*(*TORRY *nods.)*

JANELLE: What happens if no one comes?

TORRY: Well, here the policy is once a God-owner, always a God-owner 'til you die. Across the street they'll take the Gods from you if you're not takin' care of your little God.

(TORRY *comes around counter, kneels beside "dog" to pet him.*)

TORRY: Don't understand it. People take their other pets everywhere they go and no one seems to mind.

JANELLE: Other pets?

TORRY *(suspiciously)*: Pet sins?

JANELLE: You have a God?

TORRY: Yeah—a kennel full.

JANELLE: I mean one of your own.

TORRY *(stands and faces* JANELLE): Why would I want that when I see how other God-owners treat their Gods? I got enough problems. You wanna say yer good-byes and hand him over?

JANELLE *(picking up "dog")*: You be a good God. I'll be back to get you Sunday morning and take you to church with Mommy.

TORRY *(reaching for "dog")*: Oh, brother. C'mon, Lady—it's not like I ain't got nothin' to do.

JANELLE *(hugging "dog")*: You'll be good to him?

TORRY *(put off)*: If you really care, you'll take my advice: Keep the God and lose the boyfriend.

(*Pause.* JANELLE *sighs and turns over the "dog" to* TORRY, *who takes the "dog" and begins to exit.*)

JANELLE: Don't cry, God. It'll be all right. Mommy will be back soon. Oh, m'am? Where do I pay?

(TORRY *stops, turning to face* JANELLE.)

TORRY: You'll pay on your way out. Trust me!

(*Both exit*)

Who's to Blame?

Theme: The abuses and absurdities of a victim mentality

Cast:

Mr. Freeman: *35+ male; trial lawyer specializing in civil suits; corporate mind-set, upwardly mobile, and very politically correct*

Marge Blackwell: *25+ female; Mr. Freeman's secretary*

Mr. Simon: *18+ male; disgruntled brother trying to cash in on a compassionate father's foibles (prodigal son's brother in Luke 15:11-32)*

Mr. Horvitz: *35+ male; janitor at an investment company; simple-minded and big-hearted (man who received the one talent in Matthew 25:14-30)*

Mr. Mendoza: *30+ male; Mexican immigrant; common laborer (man who worked all day for a day's wage in Matthew 20:1-16)*

Setting: The office of Mr. Freeman, an attorney in a metropolitan law office. Necessary set pieces include a desk and two chairs. All other props and set pieces for desired effects only.

Running Time: 6-8 minutes

(As the scene opens, Mr. Freeman *is making a few notes with his secretary,* Marge Blackwell.*)*

Freeman: . . . and I need you to call Mr. Dishowitz today.

Marge: He's the disgruntled property owner?

Freeman: Right. The guy who lost the fig tree. Tell him we need an eyewitness; someone who actually saw the man touch the tree and curse it . . . whatever.

Marge: What about the DNA report and the lab analysis on the fingerprints?

Freeman: Negative.

Marge: That's odd.

Freeman: How many in the waiting room?

Marge: Three. Files are on your desk.

Freeman *(picks up files, peruses them):* Let's see, disgruntled son.

Marge: Older of two brothers, something about a family inheritance.

Freeman: Then there's the investor . . .

MARGE: Actually, he's the janitor who worked for an investment company. He claims they tricked him.

FREEMAN: And this Mr. . . . Mendoza?

MARGE: Immigrant. Green card. Worked all day for some vineyard worker in the valley and wanted to lodge a labor grievance.

FREEMAN: Ethnically motivated?

MARGE: I don't think so . . . it's a strange case. Either the vineyard owner isn't very smart, or he's very generous. But I don't think Mr. Mendoza has a case.

FREEMAN: Well, I need to push them through quickly this morning if I'm going to make my tee time for that charity golf event. Send in Mr. . . . . *(looking at files again)* Simon.

(MARGE exits offstage through "office door" and MR. SIMON enters. MR. FREEMAN crosses to door to greet him with a handshake.)

FREEMAN: Ah, Mr. Simon. Welcome. Such a dapper-looking outfit. Please have a seat. Can I get you something to drink? Cappuccino, mineral water . . . soda?

SIMON: No thanks.

FREEMAN: I've read your report concerning the estate of your father. Why don't you just give me a quick summary in your own words?

SIMON: Well, this all started when my younger brother, Joey, asked for his share of the inheritance.

FREEMAN: In all fairness to Joey, Mr. Simon, this is hardly his fault. His attention-getting tactics are classic responses to your father's dysfunctional behavior. Tell me, is your mother a little overbearing?

SIMON: Let's just keep my mother out of this.

FREEMAN *(writing on a notepad)*: Hmmmm. Noted.

SIMON: The point is, he wasted his inheritance and now I want to get mine before he gets his hands on that too.

FREEMAN: Oh, we'll do much better than your inheritance, Mr. Simon. We're going after the farm . . . so to speak.

SIMON: What do you mean?

FREEMAN: Well, the report says that your father clothed your brother in designer originals and furs and instructed his "servants" to kill the fatted calf.

SIMON: So?

FREEMAN: You can testify to that?

SIMON: Sure.

FREEMAN *(quirky laugh)*: Furs and slaves won't set well with a jury filled with animal rights activists and the proponents of child labor laws.

SIMON: What are you going to do?

FREEMAN: Given the situation, we paint a picture of your father as mentally unstable with a history of physical and verbal abuse from drunken parents . . .

SIMON: Yeah. The whole time my brother was gone, he was like a space man . . . just sitting at the window and staring down the road.

FREEMAN: Sounds like incompetence to me. We'll claim negligent infliction of emotional distress, tort of outrage, fraud, and discrimination. We'll sue for compensatory damages and stack fines for violation of a myriad of labor laws. He'll be forced to sell the farm to survive the financial blow *or* just turn it over to you.

SIMON: That's great.

FREEMAN *(getting up out of his chair):* Why don't you start to draft up some business proposals . . . how you would do things "differently" with the farm. *(Walking* SIMON *toward door)* We might even want to turn part of the farm into a wildlife refuge. It would show good intent on your part.

SIMON *(shaking hands):* Thanks, Mr. Freeman.

FREEMAN: No problem. Here at Freeman and Sons our motto is "You deserve more!"

*(*SIMON *nods with a smile and exits.* MR. FREEMAN *shakes his head and rolls his eyes, then turns and walks back to desk to pick up the next file. As he turns,* MR. HORVITZ *enters.)*

FREEMAN: Mr. Horvitz. Welcome. Such a dapper-looking outfit. Please have a seat. Can I get you something to drink? Cappuccino, mineral water . . . soda?

*(*MR. HORVITZ *breaks out in sobs.)*

FREEMAN *(handing him a tissue):* What's the matter, Mr. Horvitz?

MR. HORVITZ: Mineral water.

MR. FREEMAN: Mineral water?

MR. HORVITZ: I took care of changing the bottles in the water dispenser.

MR. FREEMAN: Oh . . . Why don't you tell me what happened?

MR. HORVITZ: The boss took a vacation. He called me into his office with two other guys, higher-ups, and he gave us some money to take care of while he was gone.

MR. FREEMAN: And what did you do with it?

MR. HORVITZ: I took it home and put it under my bed with the rest of my money.

MR. FREEMAN: That was . . . uh, safe.

MR. HORVITZ: I didn't know he wanted me to invest it. I mean, I'm the janitor.

MR. FREEMAN: So that wasn't made clear to you?

MR. HORVITZ: No.

MR. FREEMAN: You didn't sign anything that day?

MR. HORVITZ: Just the bathroom logs when I punched out.

MR. FREEMAN: What did he do when he came back?

MR. HORVITZ: Well, the other two guys got 100 percent returns on their money. Commodes or something like that?

MR. FREEMAN: Commodities?

MR. HORVITZ: That's it. I don't understand that stuff. I'm just the . . .

MR. FREEMAN: The janitor . . . yes, I know. Did you consider a bank account insured by the FDIC?

MR. HORVITZ: Listen, I come from a family that had to scrounge and save every penny just to make ends meet. We didn't take chances with what little we had.

MR. FREEMAN: Of course. I didn't mean to minimize your experience, Mr. Horvitz. You are an exploited proletarian.

MR. HORVITZ: I am?

MR. FREEMAN: A product of the economic system that marginalized you.

MR. HORVITZ: Really?

MR. FREEMAN: My guess is this whole thing was a conspiracy to get you fired.

MR. HORVITZ: You think?

MR. FREEMAN: Better yet, we'll prove that in court. We'll sue for the mental anguish, discrimination, intentional infliction of emotional distress, entrapment, and we'll ask the court for punitive damages and payment for pain and suffering and impaired earnings power.

MR. HORVITZ: All of that?

MR. FREEMAN: Here at Freeman and Sons, "You deserve more!"

MR. HORVITZ: What should I do?

MR. FREEMAN: Wait till you hear from me. My people will call your people, and we'll do lunch.

(MR. FREEMAN *begins walking* MR. HORVITZ *toward the door.*)

MR. HORVITZ: My people?

MR. FREEMAN: Have a great day, Mr. Horvitz.

(MR. FREEMAN *puts his hand into his head and shakes it woefully. He heads back over to the desk to pick up another folder.* MR. MENDOZA *enters.*)

MR. FREEMAN: Mr. Mendoza. Que pasa! Such a dapper-looking outfit. Please have a seat. Can I get you something to drink? Cappuccino, mineral water . . . soda?

MR. MENDOZA: No, gracias.

MR. FREEMAN: Mr. Mendoza, let me get right to the point. I've read your complaint, and I don't think you have a case here . . . yet.

MR. MENDOZA: Yet?

MR. FREEMAN: Let me get this straight. You're on welfare and living in the projects, right?

MR. MENDOZA: Si.

MR. FREEMAN: Mr. Rothmore approaches you and offers you a day's work for a day's wage?

MR. MENDOZA: Si.

MR. FREEMAN: You work the day, and he pays you accordingly.

MR. MENDOZA: Si.

MR. FREEMAN: But others, hired later in the day . . . *(looking at file)* 12:00, 3:00, and 5:00, receive the same wage for working a significantly shorter workday.

MR. MENDOZA: Si.

MR. FREEMAN: Well, Mr. Rothmore may not be motivated by profit, but he is not a criminal. I cannot see that this incident was culturally insensitive or ethnically motivated. My advice to you then is to show up at the vineyard tomorrow at 5 P.M. If he won't hire you then or fails to pay equal wages, come back and see me.

MR. MENDOZA: Si.

(As MR. MENDOZA *gets up to leave,* MARGE *reenters the office.* MR. MENDOZA *exits.)*

MR. FREEMAN: Have a nice day, Mr. Mendoza.

MARGE: We have a problem.

MR. FREEMAN: What's that?

MARGE: There's a man out here offering to settle accounts with your clients.

MR. FREEMAN: What?

MARGE: He says he's willing to pay for everything.

MR. FREEMAN: Does he appear . . . *(makes faces and signs for "crazy".)*

MARGE *(shaking her head):* He did make some kind of reference to being rich in spirit, though.

MR. FREEMAN: Hmmph. What did he come here for anyway?

MARGE: Claims he's the Son of God.

MR. FREEMAN *(incredulously):* What did you say his name was again?

MARGE: Jesus *(looks at her clipboard)* . . . ah, of Nazareth.

MR. FREEMAN: Wait a minute. *(Runs to desk, picks up and opens file folder)* Hey! That's the name of the accused in the Dishowitz civil suit.

MARGE: The guy with the fig tree?

MR. FREEMAN: You got it. Get ready to take down some notes. We're going to crucify this guy. *(As he heads out the door with* MARGE *behind him.)* Jesus, is it? Welcome. Such a dapper-looking outfit. Please have a seat. Can I get you something to drink? Cappuccino, mineral water . . . soda?

(Freeze/Dim lights)

Red Velvet

Theme: Relationships/aging

Scripture: "Honor your father and your mother, so that you may live long in the land the LORD your God is giving you" (Exodus 20:12).

Cast:

MARY: *a woman in her mid-50s*
SHIRLEY: *Mary's mother; a woman in her mid-70s*

Setting: The kitchen of a home. A table with two chairs will be sufficient. The table is neatly arranged with a small centerpiece, two cups of tea on saucers, creamer, sugar bowl, some spoons, and a napkin holder. There might also be a newspaper in the corner or a small stack of mail.

Running Time: 5 minutes

(As the scene opens MARY *is pouring a cup of tea for herself and* SHIRLEY. SHIRLEY *is browsing through a pamphlet.)*

SHIRLEY: I don't know.

MARY: I like the pink.

SHIRLEY: Just so many choices.

MARY: You look good in pink.

SHIRLEY: The red velvet was nice. You said so . . . on the way out.

MARY: It's too expensive. You know Dad would agree.

SHIRLEY: He's not going to see me in it.

MARY: People are only going to see you in it once.

SHIRLEY: It's my big night out, and I want to go out in style.

*(*SHIRLEY *reaches for the sugar.* MARY *grabs it before she gets to it and moves it out of her reach.)*

MARY: You know you can't have that.

SHIRLEY: I hate my tea without sugar.

MARY: Your diabetes . . .

SHIRLEY: I'll die happy with sugar in my veins.

MARY: Well, I'll never have a moment's rest if I let you die at my kitchen table.

*(*SHIRLEY *takes a sip of her tea and grimaces.)*

SHIRLEY: Well at least you'll have a casket to bury me in. *(Picking up the brochure again)* Honestly, whatever happened to a simple pine box? All these . . . *(Shakes her head)* Won't need any of it where I'm going. *(Closes the brochure and sets it on the table. Pause.)* Make sure they stuff my bra for the viewing.

MARY: Mother!

SHIRLEY: That's what they did to Helen Spangler. She would have been proud. I don't want to die flat-chested.

MARY: You talk about this a lot lately.

SHIRLEY: About being flat-chested?

MARY: No, about dying.

SHIRLEY: I'm not afraid of it. I just thought I'd do it my way for once. But, I didn't think there would be this many choices. I was never good with choices . . . let your father decide things. *(Reaches for milk and starts to pour some in her tea. Pauses to study milk dispenser.)* Maybe I'll get creamed.

MARY *(reaching over table to take pitcher from her)*: That's enough. *(Pause)* What would I do with your ashes?

SHIRLEY: Sprinkle them in your garden.

MARY: Like we used to do with the ashes in the potbellied stove?

SHIRLEY: That way I can live on as a carrot.

MARY: What?

SHIRLEY: Sprinkle a little of me in a row of radishes and when you eat your salad you can thank me.

MARY: Radishes give me heartburn. You give me heartache. Sometimes . . . only when you talk like this. *(Pause. Sips her tea.)* Jenny said I'm acting more like you the older I get.

SHIRLEY: You said you'd never be like me.

MARY: I know. God has a sense of humor.

SHIRLEY: How's that?

MARY: Sending you here to live after Daddy died instead of you going to live with Tom. It was no big secret you liked him better when we were growing up.

SHIRLEY: Don't start this again.

MARY: It's all right. We've had a chance to become friends again these last several months. I've enjoyed "mothering" you.

SHIRLEY *(picking up brochure)*: Is that why you want me to buy the casket with the pink silk instead of the red velvet?

MARY: What?

SHIRLEY: You're getting even with me for your senior prom?

MARY *(smiling):* I haven't thought about that for a long time. You made me wear that ugly pink taffeta dress.

SHIRLEY: Your father said we couldn't afford the red velvet.

MARY: It was my big night out. I wanted to go out in style.

SHIRLEY *(looking far away):* I wasn't good with choices.

MARY: When I got to the prom that night, Mary Ellen Newby and Jo Rose were *both* wearing the same red velvet dress. I was so glad I was in pink taffeta.

SHIRLEY: You never told me that. (MARY *hands sugar bowl to* SHIRLEY.)

MARY: Just a little.

(SHIRLEY *closes brochure and reaches across table to take* MARY'S *hand.)*

SHIRLEY: You know, I think the pink will be just fine.

(They look at each other and smile.)

Lost Keys on the High Seas

Theme: Prayer

Scripture: "Do not be anxious about anything, but in everything, by prayer and petition, with thanksgiving, present your requests to God. And the peace of God, which transcends all understanding, will guard your hearts and your minds in Christ Jesus" (Philippians 4:6-7).

Cast:
> MAN: *business traveler/sales representative*
> WOMAN: *housewife*

Setting: A kitchen, with a table and a few chairs. There is a newspaper on the table and perhaps a centerpiece, other books, etc. A smaller table/phone stand is SR of the table. A third table/stand has a tape/CD player and perhaps a few other administrative items.

Running Time: 5 minutes

(As the scene opens, MAN *is standing in the kitchen sorting through some papers. Calls offstage.)*

MAN: I'm headed out, honey.

WOMAN *(offstage):* What time does your plane leave?

MAN: I already told you—2:15.

*(*WOMAN *enters.)*

WOMAN: Better get going. You don't want to be late.

MAN *(exiting):* I'll see you on Monday.

*(*WOMAN *sits at table and opens newspaper lying there.* MAN *reenters.)*

MAN: Forgot my keys. *(Exits.* WOMAN *rolls her eyes and shakes her head.* MAN *calls from offstage.)* Honey, have you seen my keys?

WOMAN *(not looking up):* No. *(Gets up to turn on tape player. Music is the sound of waves hitting a shore—more soothing than annoying or disturbing. Returns to seat.)* Did you check your pants pockets?

MAN *(offstage):* Yeah.

WOMAN: Look in your office?

MAN *(offstage):* Not there, either.

31

WOMAN: Did you leave them under the seat in the car?

(MAN *enters and passes through to other exit.*)

MAN: We really need to get a key rack over the phone. *(Exits)*

WOMAN *(under her breath):* How long have I heard that?

(*Pause. Music on tape is starting to get rougher and more turbulent.* MAN *reenters.*)

MAN: They're not there.

WOMAN: Not under the seat?

MAN: I looked there. Are they in your purse?

WOMAN: I don't have them.

MAN *(sharply):* Would you look and see?

(WOMAN *exits.* MAN *looks around phone and grumbles, rubs head, begins to panic.* WOMAN *renters with purse.*)

WOMAN: They're not in here.

MAN: I'm not surprised. Well they just didn't grow legs and walk away.

WOMAN *(looking around the room):* When did you have them last?

MAN: When I came in from my meeting last night. *(Snide undertone)* I can't get in here without them.

WOMAN *(catching offhanded remark):* If I weren't here by myself all the time, I wouldn't have to lock the doors.

MAN: I hate having to keep these doors locked. *(Exits)*

WOMAN: OK, where did you go once you came in last night?

Man *(offstage):* I don't remember.

WOMAN *(offhandedly):* Like our anniversary last week.

(*Sound of storm on tape is beginning to pick up, the waves starting to pound the shore, which causes the actors to lose their balance now and again.* MAN *reenters with a yellow slicker on. He hands another one to her.*)

MAN: You better take this. It looks like it's going to be rough.

WOMAN *(putting on yellow raincoat):* Did you pray?

MAN: Nah. I didn't want to wake the Master.

(*Sound of lightning is heard in or around this point [either added over top of tape or timed with the effects to script]. The storm sends both of them sliding to one side of the stage.*)

MAN *(yelling over sound effects):* I'm not going to make my flight if I don't find those keys!

WOMAN: Where's the extra set I made for you?

MAN *(pulling hood up on his jacket):* I lost them.

WOMAN *(pulling hood up on her jacket):* You are so irresponsible!

MAN: Look who's talking! How many times have we had to drive back to a restaurant or a hotel to get the glasses *you* left behind . . .

(SFX: Thunder.)

WOMAN: All right! Think! Where did you go when you came in last night?

MAN *(retracing steps):* I came in and I . . . went straight to the bedroom. You were asleep . . . as usual. So I went into my office to do some work.

WOMAN: As usual.

(Another "gust of wind" or thunder clap sends them into the table.)

MAN: Hold on! *(Both grab table at opposite ends.)*

WOMAN: Wake the Master!

MAN: He shouldn't be bothered.

WOMAN: We're not going to make it! *(A wave sends her sprawling across the floor)* Whoooahhh!

MAN *(reaching):* Master! Help. Please show me where those keys are!

(Storm stops abruptly. They both respond. MAN *goes to the* WOMAN, *helping her get up. Awkward silence.* WOMAN *sniffles.)*

MAN: Are you all right?

WOMAN: Yeah. I think. Do you have a Kleenex?

MAN *(reaching in pocket to grab a Kleenex):* Yeah, I think I . . . *(Pulls out keys from the jacket pocket)* My keys!

WOMAN: Those are your spares! *(Beat)* We should have asked sooner.

MAN *(shaking head, a little ashamedly):* I know. I have to . . .

WOMAN *(taking off jacket):* I know . . . go.

*(*MAN *takes off jacket and hands it to* WOMAN. *Crosses to exit but stops and turns toward her.)*

MAN: When I get back on Monday, let's get away for a couple of days.

WOMAN *(nodding):* Sounds good. (MAN *exits. She hangs the coats over the chairs as she straightens up. She slumps back down in her seat and places her hand on the paper to rearrange it. She feels something lumpy under the paper and lifts it up. She picks up the second set of keys.)*

WOMAN: Peace, be still.

My Poor Scivivitz

Theme: Healing; God answers prayer; grumbling

Scripture: "O Jerusalem, Jerusalem, you who kill the prophets and stone those sent to you, how often I have longed to gather your children together, as a hen gathers her chicks under her wings, but you were not willing" (Matthew 23:37).

Cast:
>ANNA: *older, middle-age Jewish woman with decidedly Yiddish (Yonkers) accent*
>DRUSCILLA: *same as Anna*
>MAN
>WOMAN
>BOY
>GIRL

Setting: The well near the town of Bethany, around the year 32-33 A.D.

Running Time: 3 minutes

(Two women, ANNA and DRUSCILLA [could easily be MAURY and SID] are talking to each other at the well.)

ANNA: Druscilla, how are you?

DRUSCILLA: Not good.

ANNA: Go on, I'm listening.

DRUSCILLA: It's my Scivivitz.

ANNA: Where does it hurt?

DRUSCILLA: All over.

ANNA: Are you taking anything?

DRUSCILLA: Yes.

ANNA: Good.

DRUSCILLA: But it's not working.

ANNA: Not good.

(BOY comes running past them. He is yelling to the masses as he goes by.)

BOY: I can walk. I can walk. Jesus has made me well. He healed my crippled legs. Praise Yahweh! *(Exits)*

(Beat)

ANNA: You should not run around in your bare feet with Scivivitz.

DRUSCILLA: Why? It's not contagious.

ANNA: Not for me; for you. It's not good. Have you seen a physician?

DRUSCILLA: No. The rabbi has given me some remedies.

ANNA: Rabbi Schmabbie. What does he know about Scivivitz? He should know the Talmud so well.

DRUSCILLA: He told my husband, Abner, that I should wear a linen bag around my neck filled with the ashes of an ostrich egg.

ANNA: This is a curse, not a cure.

DRUSCILLA: He said it would ward off the evil forces.

ANNA: Evil Schmeevil. Butter wouldn't melt in your mouth.

MAN *(enters on the run. He is euphoric.)*: I can see. I can see. I was blind, but the man named Jesus touched my eyes and made me well. It's a miracle. I can see. *(Exits)*

(Beat)

DRUSCILLA: It could be worse, Anna.

ANNA: How?

DRUSCILLA: You could have Flavoistas.

ANNA: Like dear Sarah?

BOTH *(shaking heads)*: May she rest in peace.

DRUSCILLA: I thought she died of shruka in her placoistink?

ANNA: Flavoistas. This I know.

DRUSCILLA: I forget! Someday you'll be as old as me and you'll forget everything too. Then you can remember I told you this.

WOMAN *(running through)*: Jesus touched my ears. I can hear again. Listen to me. I can hear! I can hear everything. *(Exits)*

(Beat)

DRUSCILLA: So what about lunch next Tuesday?

ANNA: Tuesday?

DRUSCILLA: Lunch.

ANNA: I can't.

DRUSCILLA: Why not?

ANNA: I can't say.

DRUSCILLA: To me? What could be so bad?

ANNA: I'm going to see the doctor.

DRUSCILLA: Anna?

ANNA: They found a rash. It's a precaution.

DRUSCILLA: Do you think?

ANNA: Don't even say the word.

DRUSCILLA: Which word?

ANNA: I know what you're thinking.

DRUSCILLA: You do?

ANNA: Phlaginkush.

DRUSCILLA: I shudder at the thought.

ANNA: Just a precaution.

GIRL (running through): I'm healed. Imagine! Me a leper, and now look at me. I'm healed! Praise Yahweh. (Exits)

DRUSCILLA: All this talk of sickness has made me sad.

ANNA: We could have stayed home and read Job.

DRUSCILLA: With medicine being what it is, we should not have to worry.

ANNA: We can be sad . . . together.

DRUSCILLA: Misery loves company. Right? Of course, right!

ANNA: Soon the Messiah will come and we will be rid of pain.

DRUSCILLA: That it could be today.

ANNA: Yes. Today. (They exit together.)

Faith, South Dakota

Theme: Faith

Scripture: "Faith is being sure of what we hope for and certain of what we do not see" (Hebrews 11:1).

Cast:

Dot: *60-ish, simple and folksy, worn and warm*

Setting: The dining room of an old farmhouse. But the only thing left in the room is a single box that is strong enough to sit on. It must contain a few pictures in frames.

Running Time: 4 minutes

(As scene begins, Dot's voice is heard offstage.)

Just a couple more boxes in the dining room. Could you give me a hand with them?

(Dot enters and points offstage toward audience while directing conversation to someone who is behind her.)

Let's rest for a second. I've got to sit down. *(Sits and pulls out kerchief to wipe brow)* This pickin' up and movin' is for the birds.

(Points to audience area)

That's it right there. Last one. *(Smiles)* That's the one we've been looking for. *(Laughs)* That's what my grandpa used to say before he'd pick up the last bale of hay from the wagon and throw it into the barn. I'd always giggle, 'cause that meant we were done for the day and headed in for some of Grandma's freshly squeezed lemonade. *(Shakes head)* So many memories growin' up here. Good and bad . . . livin' off the land to survive made us stronger. We trusted God. He never let us down.

I'd offer you a chair, but we got rid of them at the yard sale. Sold just 'bout everything. Gave the rest away. Hard to believe everything we own is in boxes. The sum part of my best years in the back of an '82 Chevy pickup. Kept just enough money to drive across the country and start again. *(Laughs)* We started here with nothing, and we did all right. Lord provides.

Hmmm? Where? Going to South Dakota. Little town called Faith. Faith, South Dakota. Ever heard of it? We're going to work with the children on an Indian reservation. Lord told us to go, so . . .

I love kids. You have any? *(Listens and nods)* Hmmm. We have three. *(She opens up the box she's sitting on and pulls out a picture in a frame.)* The blond one is Melody. She's blonde like her daddy . . . well, like he used to be when he had hair. Margaret is the redhead. We don't know where that came from. I always told her it was the spitfire in her soul bubblin' up to the top of her head. She caused us fits from the day we brought her home with colic. She kept me on my knees in prayer all her growin' up years. Looking back on it, I suppose that's why the Lord allowed us to have her at all. See, I don't mind tellin' ya, I had some medical problems as a child and was never supposed to be able to have children. But God said we'd have our own. I just thought we'd adopt, which was fine with me. When I got pregnant with the first, I didn't believe it. I was afraid, I suppose, because the doctors had said I couldn't have children. I wondered if that's why we lost him at three months into the pregnancy. It was a boy, I mean, I felt sure it was. Liked to broke me. I wrestled with God then. But God spoke softly to me one night that He'd tend to the boy till we came and got him. We named him Jacob. God is so good.

(Looks down at box, pulls out another picture.)

Now here's a picture. *(Laughs)* My favorite. See it? *(Holds the picture in a frame up for the audience to see. It's black.)* You have to look very close . . . with eyes that really see. *(Pointing)* This is me about here . . . and next to me . . . right next to me, mind ya, with his arm around my shoulder is Ronald Reagan. *(Pause)* Of course, *the* Ronald Reagan, when he was the president of the United States Ronald Reagan. My husband and I went to this big political shindig in Chicago, and he was there. Oh, it's a long story, but I ended up in the same room with him. I knew I would because God had said . . . *(Stops and laughs.)* I know I must sound like a crazy old woman, but my guess is that God talks to anyone who'll listen. Anyway, since God said it, I put my camera in my purse with a brand-new roll of film and when I saw him just standin' there, I grabbed my husband and walked right up to him and asked for his picture. He said, "Sure. What's your name?" *(Stops and looks deadpan at the audience. Shakes her head.)* I couldn't remember. I couldn't remember my name. *(Laughs)* I'll never forget that. We both laughed. So, I'm next to him here and he has his arm around me like this *(Demonstrates)* and we both smile. My husband counts 1, 2, 3 . . . click. Nothing. I mean, no flash. So, Ronald Reagan says, would you like to try it again just in case? *(Looks deadpan again)* Turns out the battery was dead. *(Shakes her head)* Of course, I had the pictures developed anyway, but they didn't turn out. Still, I *know* that's me there with the president of the United States of America, Ronald Reagan. It's my favorite picture. My whole life was just like that picture . . . *(Puts it back in the box)*

Well, back to work. *(Picks up box)* Hmmm? Of course I'll miss this old place. *(Looks around)* Grew up here. Raised my children here. Everything I know, I learned here. But God says, go . . . so. *(Stops)* Besides, I like the sound of this new place. Faith, South Dakota. Faith . . . Sounds like home to me.

The Box

Theme: God wants to bless us with more than we could ever want or imagine.

Scripture: "Now to him who is able to do immeasurably more than all we ask or imagine, according to his power that is at work within us . . ." (Ephesians 3:20).

Cast:

WOMAN: *mid-50s*

Running Time: 3-4 minutes

(WOMAN *enters SL. She is dressed for housework and carries a nondescript, unmarked cardboard box. As she crosses DS into the scene, she begins to speak to the audience as if they were neighbors or old friends.*)

You're not going to believe this . . . (*Sets box down on the floor and pulls up a chair behind it*) I was rooting through some things in the attic; I normally do this during the holidays and then take some things down to the Thrift Store or the Goodwill trailer. Anyway, I ran across this box. Don't know how I missed it all these years. Look at this stuff . . . (*Starts to pull out a few mugs and then decides otherwise*) Wait. I think you'll appreciate this more if I tell you the story first.

I know you've heard me say more than once how tough things were growing up. Fred and I didn't come out of a lot of money. After we'd been married a couple years and Fred decided to start his own accounting firm, we had to scrape and pinch and save every penny; and by then, we already had three girls. Needless to say, things were tight. But we made it. There always seemed to be enough to get by on and anything extra was socked away for the ol' rainy day. Looking back on it, I just see how faithful God was to provide for us. That's really the point. God was so faithful to meet every need in the unexpected places. Anyway, so now the girls are grown up and have families of their own and Fred and I decided to invest some of that money we'd been savin'. Turns out to be enough to buy a condominium on . . . I still can't believe it . . . Sannibelle Island, off the Gulf Coast of Florida. (*Laughs*) Sannibelle Island! It's just so far beyond what I ever imagined or dreamed. I mean, look at this stuff . . . (*Begins to pull out a few items in the box*) Mismatched mugs . . . burnt orange tablecloth . . . salt and pepper shakers . . . some odds and ends flatware . . . nothing sentimental here. It was all stuff with plenty of use. So, I put it away in a box. We thought maybe, just maybe, we'd eventually get a place to take our grandchildren. You know . . . a cabin near a lake where we could all get away. Just an incredibly vague "wouldn't it be nice if . . ." thing. (*Laughs*)

You see it! *(Holds up a couple of mugs.)* This is the best I could dream . . . and even that was a step forward from where we had both come from. Never in my wildest dreams would I have thought of a condominium on Sannibelle Island. That's not for people like *me!* They wear necklaces with 14-karat gold pelicans carrying around a diamond in their mouths. I don't belong *there!* *(Shakes head)*

Only God could have done this. *(Starts to repackage the items in the box)* I tell you, it was just like Christmas for me. *(Pauses and reflects momentarily)* You know, it *is* just like Christmas; Advent, I mean. God gave us so much more than we could have ever expected. A baby . . . *(Looks down at box)* In a wooden box—born in Bethlehem to a couple not much different from Fred and me, I suppose. That baby was a seed to a future hope and a *home* more glorious than we could ever dream or imagine. *(Stands with box in her arms)* Hmmm. Only God could have done this! What a gift! *(Exits)*

Victory Report

Theme: Depression; suffering. Our God is in the midst of *all* our circumstances.

Scripture: "Though you have made me see troubles, many and bitter, you will restore my life again; from the depths of the earth you will again bring me up" (Psalm 71:20).

Cast:

WOMAN: *mid-20s; housewife*

Setting: A kitchen or laundry room with a table and chairs. The "room" should seem cluttered and a bit unkempt.

Running Time: Varies with optional endings. 5-8 minutes

Production Note: This script can be used in a variety of ways. It is written here as a *scene* that is best used in conjunction with a sermon on such topics as doubt, depression, anxiety, frustration, or other like topical issues of human struggle. However, the end of the script provides optional endings that turn it into more of a sketch that can stand alone as a dramatic ministry vehicle. One optional ending provides musical interlude if a soloist (second person) is available for ministry performance.

(A young WOMAN *enters a room. She has a load of laundry in a basket with a stack of mail lying on top of the clothes.)*

Christmas mail! *(Shakes head)* I just don't know if I can . . . *(Sets basket down on the floor at her feet and sits in chair. Begins sorting through mail and spots "letter.")* Ah yes, the annual bliss report from Deanna. *(Examines outside of letter thoughtfully)* Do I *really* want to know how wonderful her year was . . . *again;* mother of five straight-A children with a home business that pays for her trips to, oh, let's see . . . where to this year? London? Paris? Madrid? *(Tosses letter onto table)* Let's save it till New Year's when I'm really depressed. *(Notices next letter in pile, a newsletter from a large, prestigious ministry)* Oh, now this should cheer me up! "VICTORY REPORT." *(Sneers)* Could they just print that in bigger red letters?

(Pulls stapled newsletter open) Ah, isn't that sweet? There's Brother Ken walking the dog and smiling at his beautiful, Barbie-doll wife with her recently completed eye tucks. And, there's his perfect little son, Jimmy, and his perfect little sister, Della. Pink ruffles . . . Isn't that . . . *(Ripping up letter; sarcastically) precious. (To the tune of "Jingle Bells")* Victory, victory, vic'try all the way. *(Sigh)* You know just *once,* I'd like Brother Ken to send out a *defeat* report. *(Imagines reading from another letter)* Greetings, intercessors, friends, and sup-

port team: We want you to know the truth for once. We're tired, OK? Life hasn't been all pink ruffles this year. Actually, we're thinking about giving the whole thing up. And by the way, we really don't need the money . . . not for ministry, anyway. Just thought you might want to know that we're right at the edge and well, don't know if it might not be better to just jump and get it over with. Have a great Christmas. *(Puts letter on table)*

I'm sorry, Lord. Is it just me? Am I the only one on the planet that can't seem to get my life together? Christmas shopping, parties, church play . . . Almost everyone I know had their Christmas shopping done in June. Mary Frances Marley has all her presents hand-made, for goodness' sake, and I can't even seem to get to the store and get groceries once a week.

And if I have to listen to the choir director say "How fun!" one more time, I'm going to scream. *(Loudly)* Life isn't fun! Christmas isn't fun! Why? Why isn't Christmas fun anymore, Lord? What's the matter with me? *(Puts head in hands and pauses. Then, stands again. As she goes to set mail down on table, she notices a catalogue on top of the pile. Lets out a "hmmph" and picks it up to look at it momentarily.)*

Right! This is just what I need. "For the woman who has it all . . . limited edition, collector's series, pewter Nativity set." Shepherds, wise men, cows, sheep, donkeys . . . Look at that! No baby in the manger. Guess that comes extra. Hmmph. *(Sits down and looks at magazine cover. Then looks around room.)* Now that *would* be some good news. Please tell me You're not in that pewter manger, Lord. I need to know You're not in that kind of place; a place that's only for a few who have their acts together. I need You to be real in a world that's gone convenience and fast-food crazy. Real, like a sink full of dirty dishes and a house that never seems clean and a husband that's never there when I need him. *(Reaches for the pile of mail again and starts tossing letters onto table)* Real, like bills, bills, bills . . . This is my reality, Lord. *(Pulls out a couple of cloth diapers from laundry pile)* Cloth diapers. I'm the only woman in the world using cloth diapers. *(Throws diapers into pile and sits dejectedly on chair)* I've gotten so cynical, Lord. I want to see You in the manger with the dirt and the stink and the pain and the tears. That's what it's like down here. Please, please . . . I need You to come into this manger and bring a little light . . . please.

(As a sermon starter, the script can end here.)

Optional Ending No. 1:

(A baby cries. She looks up and faintly smiles.) Thank You, Lord.

Optional Ending No. 2:

(Sighs and reaches over to the "bliss letter." Opens and begins to read.) Dear friends: This is not going to be like most of the annual letters of good cheer you receive from so many others. Dave began having severe headaches in August. When they began to interfere with his work schedule, he went to have it checked out. The prognosis is not good. Dave has a brain tumor that seems to be enlarging slowing, but surely. Needless to say, it has been a most difficult time for us, and we desperately need your prayers of support. *(Pauses*

and sets letter down next to her) Forgive me, Lord. Please forgive me. *(Kneels next to chair and begins to pray)*

Optional Ending No. 3:

   This idea is a complement of ending No. 2 and music from Michael W. Smith's album *Christmastime* © 1998, Reunion Records. The title of the song is "Welcome to Our World," words and music by Chris Rice, © 1995, Clumsy Fly Music (ASCAP). The idea is that the woman would be about the business of folding laundry during the first two verses of the song. On the third verse, she would read (out loud) the ending as written in optional ending No. 2 and stay in an attitude of prayer for the remainder of the song. Of course, this entails that the accompaniment track is purchased and sung live as part of the presentation.

The Prodigal Pig

Theme: Nothing can separate us from the Father's love.

Scripture: "For I am convinced that neither death nor life, neither angels nor demons, neither the present nor the future, nor any powers, neither height nor depth, nor anything else in all creation, will be able to separate us from the love of God that is in Christ Jesus our Lord" (Romans 8:38-39).

Cast:

PRODIGAL PIG: *M/F, a slightly dimwitted pig who speaks with a good ol' down-on-the-farm twang*

Setting: Simply staged with a chair or a bale of hay DSC. Pig enters backing onto the stage, waving to someone offstage as if they are going away in the opposite direction.

Running Time: 4 minutes

Production Note: Minimum costume pieces can be used to depict the pig, such as a latex nose, hair band with pig ears, mask (full or half), or even some type of full-body costume. You might also want to consider farmer jeans or overalls and some type of old farm hat if you don't use the ears. The only other props to consider are a small pocket knife and a stick to whittle.

Bon Voyagee! River in yer derchies. Elvitis went insane! *(Waving)* Write when you get a chance. *(Faces audience and puts hands on hips; sighs)* He's finally a-goin' home. And none too soon, neither. Seems like a nice enough kid, just dumb as a box of hair. *(Snorts. This should be a recurring "bit." Whenever he laughs . . . at himself, mostly . . . he snorts.)* Look at him go! Soooiiieee! Guess he found what he was lookin' fer. My daddy always said, when you can't find somethin', either it's lost or you are. *(Sits down and pulls knife and stick out of his pocket, beings to whittle while speaking.)* Why does everyone have to learn the hard way? "Learn from the mistakes of others," my daddy always told me. "'Cause you can't live long enough to make 'em all yerself." He came here 'bout two weeks ago lookin' fer work. Hard times everywhere. I mean, when the cattle die standin' up, them there's hard times. *(Snorts)* I said to my friend, Wilbur, "Wilbur," I said, "somethin' 'bout that kid." Well, couple days later, pig slop started getting skimpy. Wilbur said t'was my imagination.

Now, I may not be the sharpest knife in the drawer, but I know when I'm hungry. Come to find out, the kid is dippin' into the feed! My daddy always said a stranger's business ain't your own, but this kid was eatin' my food and workin' in my pen. Way I figured it, he was family, just like Wilbur, Mort, and the others. Soooiiieee! I was hotter than pot roast. Wilbur, he said that I needed to talk to the boy first, 'cause you can't weigh the facts if the scales are loaded down with your opinions. That Wilbur, he's a smart pig . . . just like my daddy. Kind of got his antennae pickin' up all the channels, if ya know what I mean. *(Snorts)*

So, this mornin', that boy comes in with our food and I ask him, "Boy, you been diggin' in the slop?" He liked to rolled over in the mud and died. But, I figured somethin' needed sayin'. Oh, he denied it, acting like it wasn't him, just the drought. I asked him if he thought I'd just fallen out of the stupid tree and hit every branch on the way down. That sort of lightened him up a bit, and we started talkin'.

Before long, he was tellin' us his whole life story. Soooiiieee. Seems he'd taken off with half the family fortune and squandered all that money on wild livin'. When things got really bad, he had to take a job here just to stay alive. *(Snort)* Yup, I suppose there's a high cost to low livin'. Mort suggested he just stay put till things got better with the famine and all. That Mort's got the brains of a garden tool. *(Snorts)* Wilbur asked him why he didn't just go home and go work for his father. Kid got real sadlike with his tail between his legs and said he was too ashamed of what he'd done. *(Beat)* I liked to choked on the locust shell I was chewin' on. "You leave the peacockin' to the peacocks," I said. See, I knew a thing or two about a father's love, and if his daddy was half the pig my daddy was . . . wouldn't matter if he'd sold the farm from underneath his feet! Nothin' could separate him from his father's love. Nothin'! A good daddy forgives and forgets and forgets he forgave. *(Pause)*

Guess that's what he wanted to hear all along, 'cause he pulled himself out of the mud and right then and there said he was goin' home. Pretty smart considering all the stupid things he'd done. But then again, it's like Wilbur once told me, "When yer head's in the bear's mouth ain't the time to be smackin' him around and callin' him names!" *(Snort)*

(He turns to wave again.) Au reservoir! Have a good trip! *(He puts the knife and the stick away. He sighs.)* It feels good to help someone who's been beaten up by the world and left for dead on the side of the road. But, I guess that's another story, huh? *(Snorts and exits.)*